KU-511-521

CONTENTS

"THE POWER OF A THOUSAND SUNS"

At 8.15 AM on 6 August 1945, the USA dropped an entirely new type of bomb – the atom bomb – on the city of Hiroshima in Japan. Around 80,000 people were killed instantly, and thousands more died over the following weeks. Within days, the Second World War finally ended.

The atom bomb was the result of the scientific discovery that the atoms, or tiny particles, of certain elements could be split to release colossal amounts of power. When the scientist who led American research into the atom bomb, Robert Oppenheimer, first saw the results of an atomic explosion, he was reminded of a line from a Hindu myth: "If the power of a thousand suns were to burst at once in the sky, I would be Death, the Destroyer of worlds."

◀ **Nuclear explosion**
The nuclear bomb dropped on Hiroshima created a mushroom-shaped cloud over the city. The cloud's shape is the result of the huge vacuum created by the heat of the explosion. This vacuum sucks in debris and throws it high into the air.

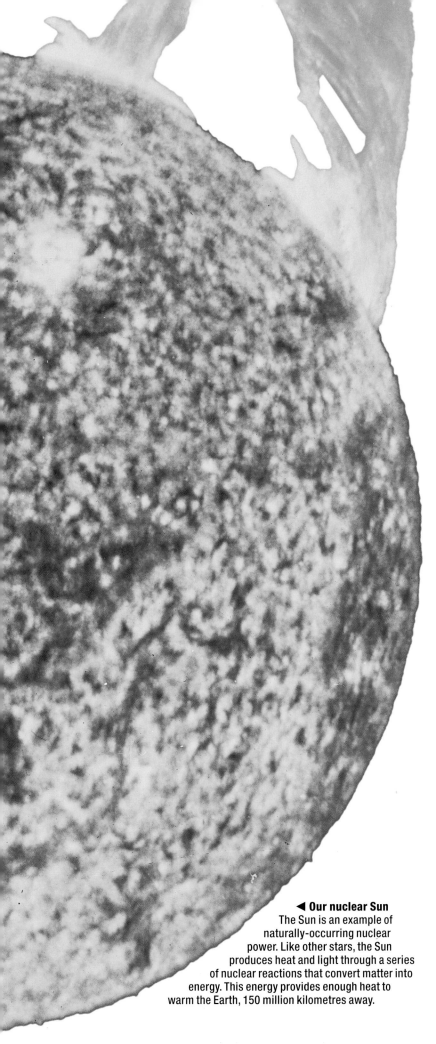

◀ Our nuclear Sun
The Sun is an example of
naturally-occurring nuclear
power. Like other stars, the Sun
produces heat and light through a series
of nuclear reactions that convert matter into
energy. This energy provides enough heat to
warm the Earth, 150 million kilometres away.

▼ Nuclear disaster, 1986
Following an accident at a nuclear
power station at Chernobyl in Russia,
hundreds of thousands were affected by
nuclear fallout, and a radioactive cloud
spread across Europe.

Positive outcomes?

The technology that was developed to
make nuclear bombs has been adapted
for peaceful uses, such as generating
electricity. However, the technology itself
continues to make many people nervous.
While nuclear energy does not produce
harmful greenhouse gases, it does have
the power to devastate large areas of the
world if not carefully controlled. And the
threat of a country or terrorist group using
a nuclear warhead is the single greatest
concern of the international community.

▼ Looking for nuclear weapons
United Nations (UN) weapons
inspectors search for evidence of
nuclear and other weapons of mass
destruction in Iraq, 2002. Fears that
Iraq may have been developing
nuclear bombs led, in part, to the
armed conflict there in 2003.

SPLITTING THE ATOM

In 1905, the German-born scientist Albert Einstein published his theory of special relativity. This said that there are huge amounts of energy locked up in atoms. Over the next thirty years, scientists in various European countries worked to put Einstein's theory into practice. They discovered that a powerful force holds together the nucleus (main part) of an atom and that, if they could split the nucleus, the energy inside it could be released.

In 1938, scientists in Germany successfully split an atom of the metal uranium, in a process known as nuclear fission. If the scientists could split one atom and ensure that the energy released broke up other atoms, it could lead to a chain reaction that would release vast amounts of power.

▲ **Roosevelt at the White House**
President Roosevelt was initially opposed to war against Germany. Under pressure, however, he agreed to set up a research group – the Uranium Committee – to explore the possibilities of nuclear power.

Einstein's warning

By 1938, the Nazis under Adolf Hitler were threatening the stability of Europe. When Einstein, now a refugee living in the USA, heard about the German breakthrough, he was extremely concerned. He feared that German scientists would be able to harness this destructive power to help the Nazis in any future war.

In August 1939, one month before the Second World War broke out, Einstein wrote a letter to the US president, Franklin D. Roosevelt. Einstein described how incredible amounts of energy could be created by splitting the uranium atom, and how this could then be used to make unimaginably powerful bombs. He urged Roosevelt to set up a nuclear research project in the USA, to beat Germany in the race to nuclear technology.

▲ **Enrico Fermi**
Enrico Fermi was an Italian Nobel-Prize winning scientist. He had been researching nuclear fission before he was forced into exile in the USA. At the University of Chicago, in December 1942, Fermi carried out the first ever controlled nuclear chain reaction.

▼ Einstein's letter to Roosevelt
In 1939, Einstein (pictured right) urged the US government to beat Germany in the race to develop nuclear weapons. In later years, Einstein deeply regretted his role in the development of such weapons.

Albert Einstein
Old Grove Rd.
Nassau Point
Peconic, Long Island

August 2nd, 1939

F.D. Roosevelt
President of the United States,
White House
Washington, D.C.

Sir:

Some recent work by E.Fermi and L. Szilard, which has been communicated to me in manuscript, leads me to expect that the element uranium may be turned into a new and important source of energy in the immediate future. Certain aspects of the situation which has arisen seem to call for watchfulness and, if necessary, quick action on the part of the Administration. I believe therefore that it is my duty to bring to your attention the following facts and recommendations:

In the course of the last four months it has been made probable – through the work of Joliot in France as well as Fermi and Szilard in America – that it may become possible to set up a nuclear chain reaction in a large mass of uranium,by which vast amounts of power and large quantities of new radium-like elements would be generated. Now it appears almost certain that this could be achieved in the immediate future.

This new phenomenon would also lead to the construction of bombs, and it is conceivable – though much less certain – that extremely powerful bombs of a new type may thus be constructed. A single bomb of this type, carried by boat and exploded in a port, might very well destroy the whole port together with some of the surrounding territory. However, such bombs might very well prove to be too heavy for transportation by air.

THE SPREAD OF WAR

The start of the Second World War made the race to develop nuclear technology all the more urgent. On 1 September 1939, Germany invaded Poland. Two days later, France and Britain declared war on Germany in an attempt to halt Hitler's plans to rule Europe. Over the next twelve months, the fighting spread through Europe, across North Africa and into the Middle East. From the other side of the Atlantic, the USA looked on anxiously.

In September 1940, Japan signed an alliance with Germany and Italy. Japan had strong ambitions to become the dominant power in Asia. It had been at war with China since 1937, and had gained some territory from the Chinese. In late 1940, Japan also began to capture British territory in Asia.

US indecision

The USA still could not decide what to do. To the east across the Atlantic, it could see that Europe was in turmoil, while to the west across the Pacific, the same was true in Asia. President Roosevelt felt a strong desire to support Britain, but was unsure about taking his country into war.

▼ Gas attack practice
This rehearsal of a gas attack took place in Tokyo in 1936. Photos such as this show that Japan had been preparing its citizens for war for a long time.

ASIA

Japan

Pearl Harbor

◄ Attack on Pearl Harbor
The US Navy's ships USS *West Virginia* and USS *Tennessee* burn after the air attack by Japanese bombers in December 1941. The attack stunned and angered Americans, and drew the United States into the Second World War.

◄ Japanese war poster
This poster shows a Samurai warrior destroying enemy ships. In Japanese history, the Samurai were warriors who were trained to defend the emperor, even if it meant their own death. This image was part of a huge propaganda campaign by the Japanese government to whip up enthusiasm for the war.

Pearl Harbor

In the end, Japan made the decision for President Roosevelt. On 7 December 1941, Japanese aircraft launched a surprise attack on one of the USA's main naval bases, at Pearl Harbor on the Hawaiian island of Oahu. More than 2,500 sailors died in the raid, which destroyed the base as well as many ships and planes. As far as the United States was concerned, the attack was a declaration of war. Britain joined the USA in declaring war on Japan. In turn, on 11 December, Germany and Italy declared war on the USA.

Facing both ways
The early stages of the Second World War centred on Europe. However, the attack on Pearl Harbor meant that the USA faced conflict on two fronts – towards Europe to its east and towards Japan and Asia to its west.

USA ➡ EUROPE

THE MANHATTAN PROJECT

▼ Nazi round-up, Germany
During the 1930s, many Jewish scientists were forced out of Nazi Germany and took refuge in the USA. Many of these scientists worked on the Manhattan Project – their contribution helped the USA to develop the nuclear bomb.

The attack on Pearl Harbor hastened the USA's entry into the war. But even before it, many Americans believed that, sooner or later, they would have to join in the conflict. Already, two months before Pearl Harbor, President Roosevelt had approved intensified research into the possibility of an atom bomb. Once the USA joined the war, making a nuclear weapon became even more important.

Research in the desert

In December 1941 the US government set up the top-secret Manhattan Project, which had the task of creating a viable atom bomb as quickly as possible. The project took its name from Manhattan in New York, where early atomic research had been carried out. Work took place across the USA, and more than 40,000 people were employed on the project.

Most of the project's scientists were gathered together at Los Alamos, a remote site in the New Mexico desert. The scientist Robert Oppenheimer was put in charge of the research, while the project's military leader, Brigadier-General Leslie Groves, surrounded the Los Alamos site with the tightest possible security. At the height of the project, 6,000 people lived and worked in the new town of Los Alamos.

A race without competitors

The race was on to develop an atom bomb. However, unknown to the USA, Germany focused most of its research on nuclear theory rather than how to make a bomb. Japan had considered making an atom bomb, but never proceeded beyond the initial research. In contrast, the USA poured vast resources – totalling some $2 billion – into the Manhattan Project.

▼ **Robert Oppenheimer**
Oppenheimer led the US project to create an atom bomb. After the war, in 1946, his work earned him the US Medal of Merit.

▼ **Los Alamos**
The Manhattan Project scientists were housed in a vast, isolated site at Los Alamos in New Mexico (main picture and inset, below). Their lives there were very restricted, and for security reasons they were expected to remain in Los Alamos for the duration of the war.

STOP

DELTA BLDG
R-117

TA1 MAIN TECH AREA

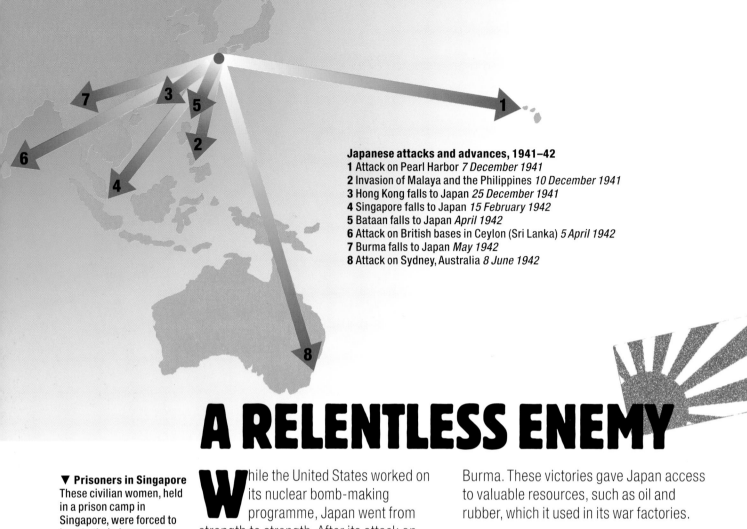

Japanese attacks and advances, 1941–42
1 Attack on Pearl Harbor *7 December 1941*
2 Invasion of Malaya and the Philippines *10 December 1941*
3 Hong Kong falls to Japan *25 December 1941*
4 Singapore falls to Japan *15 February 1942*
5 Bataan falls to Japan *April 1942*
6 Attack on British bases in Ceylon (Sri Lanka) *5 April 1942*
7 Burma falls to Japan *May 1942*
8 Attack on Sydney, Australia *8 June 1942*

A RELENTLESS ENEMY

▼ Prisoners in Singapore
These civilian women, held in a prison camp in Singapore, were forced to bow to their Japanese guards at all times. When the British colony of Singapore fell to Japan in 1942, many ordinary people were made prisoners and subjected to extremely harsh treatment.

While the United States worked on its nuclear bomb-making programme, Japan went from strength to strength. After its attack on Pearl Harbor and entry into the Second World War, Japan made the same lightning advance across Asia as Germany had achieved in Europe. Within six months Japanese forces had occupied Malaya, the Philippines, Hong Kong, Singapore and Burma. These victories gave Japan access to valuable resources, such as oil and rubber, which it used in its war factories.

Treatment of prisoners
American, British and Australasian Allied forces became engaged in a gruelling war in the Pacific against the Japanese. In many ways, this conflict was much more savage than the one fought in Europe.

▼ Japanese factory, 1941
Japan put all its industrial might into the production of huge numbers of planes and ships. By the time it provoked war with the USA in 1941, Japan was a very well-armed nation.

While the Nazis committed terrible acts against Jews, Communists and others, they tended to deal with captured soldiers in line with international law. In contrast, the Japanese treated their military prisoners very badly. Japanese traditions of honour meant that they viewed defeated soldiers with contempt. They forced prisoners to work in extremely harsh conditions; building a railway in Thailand, for example, claimed 16,000 lives.

As news of Japan's cruelty towards its prisoners of war reached the American public, as well as its leaders, hatred of the Japanese reached extreme levels.

► National pride
This photograph, taken in 1942, shows a Japanese soldier waving the national flag while Japanese warplanes fly overhead.

◄ Bataan Death March, 1942
When Bataan in the Philippines fell to Japan, thousands of US and Filipino prisoners were forced to march more than 100 kilometres to their prison camp. The prisoners suffered from intense heat, a lack of food and water, and shootings and beatings from the Japanese. Up to 10,000 men died on the march.

SLOW PROGRESS

▼ USS *Bunker Hill*

On 11 May 1945, while supporting the invasion of Okinawa, the American warship USS *Bunker Hill* was hit by two Japanese kamikaze planes. Kamikaze attacks were virtually irresistible unless the planes could be shot down. This attack killed 372 servicemen and wounded 264 more.

For six months, Japan's advance seemed unstoppable on land, at sea and in the air. Then, in June 1942, Japan suffered a setback at sea in the Battle of Midway, when the USA sank four Japanese aircraft carriers to only one American loss.

But the war was far from won. Japanese soldiers had a high degree of loyalty to their ruler, Emperor Hirohito, which meant that they were prepared to fight to the death. In 1944, Japanese military leaders started using this loyalty to stage devastating kamikaze, or suicide, attacks. Individual pilots and soldiers were chosen to fly planes, or throw themselves as human bombs, directly at the enemy.

Island-hopping

Slowly, American, British and Australasian Allied forces began to win back island after island from Japan. The fighting was tough; jungle conditions were unfamiliar to many of the soldiers, and the beach landings left the forces exposed and vulnerable. The Allied armies sustained huge losses.

In April 1945, the Allied forces reached the island of Okinawa, very close to Japan. For two months, the island witnessed a fierce battle, which the Allies eventually won, at a cost of around 100,000 Japanese and 12,000 US soldiers' lives. The victory at Okinawa gave the Allied forces a base to support operations against Japan itself.

▼ Air strikes on Tokyo

Japan's Emperor Hirohito inspects the damage caused by Allied air raids on Tokyo in 1945. The Allies' victories on outlying Japanese islands gave them bases from which to launch air strikes on Japan's main islands.

►► Japanese prisoner

Allied soldiers surround a Japanese prisoner after the Allied invasion of the Marshall Islands in the South Pacific, 1944. Allied forces treated their Japanese prisoners harshly, in retaliation for Japanese cruelty towards Allied captives.

▼ Kamikaze pilot
This young Japanese pilot was photographed in July 1944. He is holding a Samurai sword, a symbol of loyalty to the emperor. Traditions of loyalty and honour led many Japanese to sacrifice their lives on kamikaze missions.

RESEARCH CONTINUES

00:00:00.016

HOURS   MINUTES   SECONDS

TIME ELAPSED SINCE DETONATION: 0:00:0.016

0:00:0.016

0 HOURS
0 MINUTES
0.016 SECONDS

0.016 SEC.
N

100 METERS

▲ Photograph of the first test, July 1945
A fraction of a second after detonation, the bomb had created the huge fireball seen here.

▼ Before and after the test
(Below left) The bomb was dropped from a 30-metre tower, to see its effect when dropped from a plane. (Below right) The explosion melted the tower's metal structure, and turned the surrounding sand into glass-like crystals.

As war raged in Europe, Asia and elsewhere, research continued in the New Mexico desert into the development of the atom bomb. It proved extremely difficult work. It is estimated that scientists on the Manhattan Project crammed thirty years of research and development into a four-year period.

The scientists worked on two types of fission bomb that would be small enough to carry on a plane. One type used uranium; the other used plutonium. These radioactive metallic elements are "heavier", or more strongly held together, than most other elements. The scientists knew that breaking up the heaviest elements would release the most energy, creating the biggest explosion (see page 6).

Little Boy and Fat Man

The scientists named the bomb that used uranium "Little Boy". It worked by firing one piece of uranium 235 into another. (The number refers to the type of atoms in the element: uranium 235 has 235 more neutrons than protons.) They named the second bomb "Fat Man". This was a more complicated bomb, which used plutonium 239 surrounded by high explosives.

▼ The atom bombs

The two types of bomb developed by the Manhattan Project scientists were called the "Little Boy" (at the front) and the "Fat Man".

The bombs were named for their different shapes, but both had similar weights. Little Boy weighed around 4,000 kilograms, while Fat Man was approximately 4,500 kilograms.

Ready for use

By the end of 1944, General Groves, the military head of the Manhattan Project, informed President Roosevelt that the first atom bomb would be ready by the following summer. The first test (the "Trinity test") took place on 16 July 1945, at Alamogordo in the New Mexico desert. Until then, no-one had been absolutely certain that the bomb would work. The test was successful, however, and revealed an awesome power – everything nearby was simply pulverised or melted, and observers, standing over 10,000 metres away, were knocked flat.

VICTORY IN EUROPE

► **The Potsdam Conference**
Leaders of the Allied nations (from left: Britain's Winston Churchill, the USA's Harry Truman and the USSR's Joseph Stalin) met in Potsdam, Germany, in July 1945. They discussed the division of postwar Europe, as well as how to end the war in Japan.

▼ **Celebrating victory**
After Germany had surrendered, VE Day (Victory in Europe Day) celebrations were held all over Europe, like this one in Piccadilly Circus, London.

On 7 May 1945, Germany surrendered to the Allied forces. Celebrations broke out across Europe, but tension between the Allies – particularly the USA and the USSR – meant that the ongoing war in Asia remained a grave concern.

Before the Nazis had surrendered, the Allies competed with each other to capture as much of Germany as they could. As a result, many people felt that the alliance was not a product of genuine friendship or trust between nations. While they had

◄ **East meets West**
Russian and American soldiers shake hands at the River Elbe in Germany, April 1945. The early friendship between the two nations did not last long.

▼ **Flying the Soviet flag**
Victorious Russian troops seize the Reichstag, the German parliament building in Berlin, after the Nazis' surrender in May 1945.

come together to defeat a common enemy, the USA and the USSR distrusted what they believed to be each other's plans to take over as much of the world as possible.

Planning for a new world

At the same time, neither side wanted more fighting. At a conference in Potsdam, Germany in July 1945, the Allies tried to share out Europe between them. There was little concern about the views of the people in the countries being divided. The old League of Nations had collapsed and the United Nations was not yet established, so it was up to the victors to work out the shape of the postwar world.

At Potsdam, the Allies also discussed the continuing war against Japan. The USA, which was heavily engaged in fighting Japan, secured an agreement that the USSR would not enter the conflict in the Pacific until after 15 August. The United States was worried that, if the USSR joined the war against the Japanese, it would seek to gain control over the region once Japan had been defeated.

"NO GREAT DECISION"

► **Roosevelt's funeral**
The funeral procession of US president Franklin Roosevelt, 15 April 1945. Despite being crippled with polio, Roosevelt had been an outstanding president both before and during the Second World War.

▼ **Truman's inauguration**
Harry Truman delivering his first speech as US president. When he became president Truman was not very well known, but he had been heavily involved in the USA's war plans. It was his decision to drop the bomb on Japan.

By the time of the Potsdam Conference, the war in the Pacific was not going well for Japan. The Allies knew that Japan was close to surrender, but many Japanese politicians found this idea impossible to accept. Their biggest fear was that the Allies would remove Emperor Hirohito from power. Many Japanese regarded Hirohito as a god, and were afraid of what would happen to their society if he lost his power.

Allied fears

At the Potsdam Conference, the Allied leaders repeated their call for Japan to surrender unconditionally. However, many felt it would take more than words to make Japan accept defeat. The Allies feared that the war in the Pacific would continue into 1946, with the loss of many more lives on both sides. In addition, the USA was keen to defeat Japan before the USSR became heavily involved (see pages 18-19).

USSR

EUROPE

◀ **Kyoto**
Kyoto is the ancient capital of Japan. US military planners considered it as a target for the first atom bomb, along with the cities of Hiroshima, Niigata, Kokura and Nagasaki. The planners rejected Kyoto because they felt that, if it was destroyed, the Japanese might never forgive the West.

The top-secret plan

In April 1945, Franklin Roosevelt had died in office. Harry S. Truman became the new president of the United States. Truman's advisors told him about the top-secret development of the atom bomb. The president agreed with them that this would be the quickest and easiest way to finish the war. Planning began at once to select targets in Japan for the first-ever atom bomb attack.

At this point, some of the scientists on the Manhattan Project wanted to warn Japan about the attack. They even suggested dropping the bomb in a remote area to show its destructive power without killing too many people. But several of Truman's key advisors made sure that these requests did not reach the president.

Truman's conviction

Truman himself felt it was right to proceed with the plan to drop the bomb. He had three main reasons for this: firstly the bomb would bring the war to an end, secondly it would keep the USSR out of Asia, and thirdly it would test America's new technology. President Truman said afterwards that it was "no great decision" to drop the bomb.

USSR

ASIA

◀ **A pivotal position**
The USSR, like the USA (pages 8-9), faced both Europe and Asia. Unlike the USA, however, it had both continents on its doorstep. The USA feared that the USSR would try to increase its power by gaining territory in Asia.

"ENOLA GAY IS ON ITS WAY"

In the early summer of 1945, all the necessary components of the atom bombs were shipped in secret to Tinian Island, in the central Pacific, nearly 1,500 kilometres east of the Philippines.

By July, a specially-selected aircrew led by Colonel Paul Tibbets was in place on the island. On 5 August the crew's orders arrived. The next day, ground personnel loaded one of the Little Boy-type bombs onto the huge B-29 bomber, *Enola Gay*, and the crew took off for Japan. Only Colonel Tibbets knew exactly what the bomb was. The rest of the crew had been told that it was a secret weapon that might end the war. No-one knew if it would be possible to drop an atom bomb and get out of the way quickly enough for the plane's crew to survive the blast.

At the time most people were unaware of the enormous destruction that one bomb could cause. Although in Germany they had seen the effects of "blanket bombing" (extremely heavy bombardment of a city or region) with conventional bombs, they had no idea of what the intense heat and radiation of a nuclear bomb would do.

The flight

The *Enola Gay* flew in formation with two other planes towards Japan. Weather planes flew ahead of them, checking the conditions for bombing. Even at this stage, the decision had not been made about which city would be bombed. It could have been Kokura, Nagasaki or Hiroshima (see page 29). An hour before they were due to attack, Colonel Tibbets finally told the crew that they were to drop the first atom bomb.

▼ The *Enola Gay*
(Bottom) The *Enola Gay*, taking off for the first-ever nuclear bomb attack. The aircraft, a Boeing B-29 Superfortress, was named *Enola Gay* after the captain's mother.

▼ The crew
The crew of the *Enola Gay* pose by the side of their plane, with their leader, Colonel Paul Tibbets, standing in the centre. All the preparations for the mission were filmed and photographed.

"IT'S HIROSHIMA!"

▲ Prime Minister Suzuki
Suzuki was Japan's prime minister at the time of the Hiroshima attack. A weak leader, he tried to balance the forces in the Japanese government who wanted peace with those who wanted to fight on. Japan did not surrender to the Allies until after a second atom bomb attack.

As the *Enola Gay* flew towards Japan, the crew learned that their target was Hiroshima. Crews in the weather planes in front of the bomber had selected the city because it had the clearest weather conditions. When Colonel Tibbets told his men "It's Hiroshima!", the fate of the city and its inhabitants was sealed.

The bomb was dropped at exactly 8.15 AM, Japanese time. Some survivors later recalled seeing three planes and a bomb in the air. When the bomb exploded above the city, it killed about 80,000 people in a blinding flash of heat and radiation. The destruction was so complete that there was simply nothing left of many people – they had been vaporised by the heat.

"A rain of ruin"
Immediately after the attack, the USA repeated its call for the Japanese to surrender. President Truman issued a statement, which said: "If they do not now accept our terms, they may expect a rain of ruin from the air, the like of which has never been seen on this earth."

As the planes flew away from Hiroshima, one pilot said, "My God, what have we done?" Many of the scientists on the Manhattan Project celebrated the success, but later some claimed they felt physically sick when they learned how many people had died as a result of the bomb.

▶ The New York Times
Americans woke up on 7 August to news of the destruction caused by the atom bomb, the secret weapon which had been four years in the making.

All the News That's Fit to Print

The New York Times.

NEW YORK, TUESDAY, AUGUST 7, 1945

LATE CITY EDITION

THREE CENTS

VOL. XCIV. No. 31,972

FIRST ATOMIC BOMB DROPPED ON JAPAN; MISSILE IS EQUAL TO 20,000 TONS OF TNT; TRUMAN WARNS FOE OF A 'RAIN OF RUIN'

HIRAM W. JOHNSON, REPUBLICAN DEAN IN THE SENATE, DIES

Jet Plane Explosion Kills Major Bong, Top U.S. Ace

KYUSHU CITY RAZED

Kenney's Planes Blast Tarumizu in Record Blow From Okinawa

ROCKET SITE IS SEEN

125 B-29's Hit Toyokawa Naval Arsenal in Demolition Strike

REPORT BY BRITAIN

Steel Tower 'Vaporized' In Trial of Mighty Bomb

'By God's Mercy' We Beat Nazis to Bomb, Churchill Says

Scientists Awe-Struck as Blinding Flash Lighted New Mexico Desert and Great Cloud Bore 40,000 Feet Into Sky

NEW AGE USHERED

Day of Atomic Energy Hailed by President, Revealing Weapon

HIROSHIMA IS TARGET

'Impenetrable' Cloud of Dust Hides City After Single Bomb Strikes

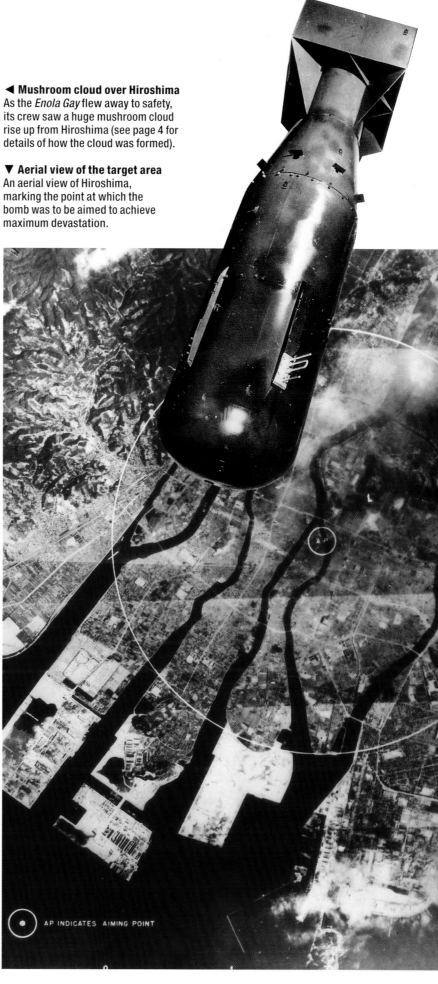

◄ Mushroom cloud over Hiroshima
As the *Enola Gay* flew away to safety, its crew saw a huge mushroom cloud rise up from Hiroshima (see page 4 for details of how the cloud was formed).

▼ Aerial view of the target area
An aerial view of Hiroshima, marking the point at which the bomb was to be aimed to achieve maximum devastation.

AP INDICATES AIMING POINT

ON THE GROUND

▼ Hiroshima before and after the bomb
(Top) Hiroshima harbour before the atom bomb was dropped.
(Bottom) Survivors walking along a street in the city after the blast. Before the devastation caused by the bomb, Hiroshima was a major centre of industry, with important transport links by sea and rail. It also had the largest number of Christians in Japan.

Before the bomb was dropped, some 300,000 people lived in Hiroshima, on the main Japanese island of Honshu. Hiroshima is on a river delta, and had been a fishing settlement for centuries. It had grown into an industrial city which helped to sustain the Japanese war effort.

Destruction beyond imagining

The atom bomb was dropped right in the middle of the city. In one blow, it flattened nearly everything for about 1.5 kilometres around the site where the bomb landed. The blast stripped trees bare. Debris from buildings was sucked into the giant mushroom cloud that formed over the city.

Approximately 80,000 people were killed in the instant of the flash, and many more died within hours from severe burns. Huge shock waves knocked over most buildings in a 10-kilometre area, crushing the people inside. Those outside were showered with debris, which ripped the skin from their bodies.

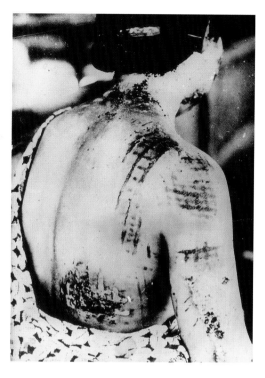

◄ A survivor
A woman shows how the bomb blast at Hiroshima has scorched the pattern of her clothes into her skin. Many people who survived the bomb were severely burned.

A huge fire consumed the city, making escape almost impossible. Many people drowned in the river, trying to get away from the flames. Many others, even those some distance from the actual bomb site, were killed by the heat from the blast.

Survivors who could still walk tried to find their way out of the city they once knew, now reduced to rubble. On all sides they saw piles of dead and dying people – sights that would haunt them forever.

▼ Aerial view after the bomb was dropped
Almost 98 per cent of Hiroshima's buildings were destroyed or severely damaged by the bomb. This photograph gives some idea of the scale of the devastation.

A SECOND BOMB

On 9 August, three days after Hiroshima was destroyed, a second atom bomb was prepared for use. This time officials chose a Fat Man-type plutonium bomb. It was loaded onto the bomber *Bock's Car* and flown to Japan.

As before, the exact target depended on the weather. The bomb was originally intended for the city of Kokura, but the weather conditions were not right. Finally, with the plane almost out of fuel, the atom bomb was dropped on the shipbuilding city of Nagasaki, on Japan's Kyushu island.

Less devastating; still deadly

Although the plutonium bomb was more powerful than the uranium one dropped on Hiroshima (see page 16), the blast was not as devastating. This was because the hills surrounding Nagasaki protected it from the full force of the explosion. However, approximately 45,000 people died almost instantly in the intense heat and strength of the blast. Many more received lethal doses of radiation that would lead to sickness and death in the following weeks. A third of the city was razed to the ground.

► **Nagasaki before and after the bomb**
(Top) A street in Nagasaki's picturesque city centre, before the blast. (Bottom) Splintered tree trunks and gutted buildings in a badly-damaged part of the city, after the bomb. The hills around the city, visible in the bottom photograph, protected Nagasaki from even worse damage.

▶ The "Fat Man" bomb
The crew of *Bock's Car* dropped a Fat Man plutonium bomb on Nagasaki. This was a more complex and powerful weapon than the bomb used on Hiroshima.

Why drop a second bomb?

Some people believe that the USA bombed a second city to find out which of the two types of bomb worked best. Others maintain that the USA bombed Nagasaki to ensure Japan's immediate surrender. The Japanese government had little time to absorb the devastation in Hiroshima before the second bomb was used. However, even after the Hiroshima attack, Japanese politicians were still arguing about the terms of the surrender. After Nagasaki, President Truman cancelled the use of a third atom bomb.

◀ The same aerial view, before and after the bomb
(Top) This aerial photograph, taken on 7 August 1945, shows the tightly-packed buildings of Nagasaki.
(Bottom) This photograph, taken from the same position five days later, reveals how few buildings remained standing after the blast. "Ground Zero", in the bottom photograph, refers to the site where the bomb landed.

▶ Japanese targets
The cities that the USA considered possible targets for the first atom bomb attacks.

Niigata

Hiroshima

Kokura

Nagasaki

Kyoto

Toyko

UNCONDITIONAL SURRENDER

▲ US checkpoint in Tokyo
A soldier stands guard at one of the entrance points for Tokyo. Soon after the Japanese surrender on 15 August, American troops began a military occupation of the country that lasted until 1952.

The Allies' demand for unconditional surrender (a complete surrender with no concessions) made it much harder for the Japanese to end the fighting. Many Japanese politicians would only agree to a surrender if Emperor Hirohito remained on the throne. To surrender totally seemed to them an insult to their ruler, and an end to their 1,000-year-old culture. The Allies, however, insisted that once Japan surrendered the emperor would have to follow orders from the occupying force.

Even after the devastation caused by the two atom bombs, some members of the Japanese government still could not agree to a surrender. Only after Emperor Hirohito was persuaded of the need for it did the government accept unconditional surrender. Finally, on 15 August, the emperor told the Japanese people in a radio broadcast that the war was over.

▼ Signing the surrender
General Douglas MacArthur (far left) witnesses the signing of the surrender by a delegation of Japan's leaders on board the USS *Missouri*, 2 September 1945.

◀ **Japanese prisoners of war**
Japanese prisoners, held by Allied forces on the Pacific island of Guam, bow their heads in shame after hearing the news of Japan's surrender. With their strong tradition of military honour, the Japanese found defeat and surrender particularly hard to accept.

▼ **Allied prisoners of war**
Allied prisoners of war celebrate their liberation from Changi prison camp, August 1945. Survivors of the Japanese camps told terrible stories of starvation, disease and mistreatment.

The effects of surrender

Japanese military leaders were genuinely shocked and stunned by their country's surrender. Many ordinary people, however, were resigned to the defeat. One reason for this was that a blockade of Japanese ports by US warships had left the economy on the verge of collapse. Most people hoped that, after the surrender, their living conditions would improve.

Shortly after the emperor's declaration, Allied forces arrived in Japan. One of their first tasks was to liberate prisoners of war. The Japanese imprisoned more than 100,000 soldiers during the war, and many of them had died in captivity. The survivors were suffering the effects of malnutrition, disease and the cruelty of their captors. They were treated on US hospital ships before beginning their journeys home.

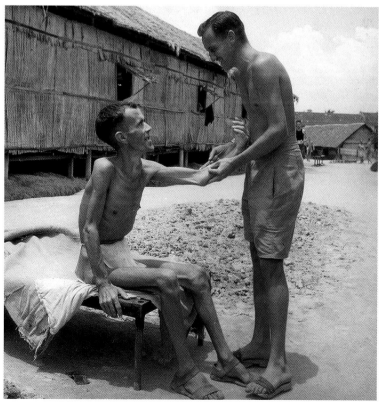

AFTER THE SURRENDER

After the surrender, Allied forces moved in to occupy Japan. They would remain there for nearly seven years. The occupation was led by the USA, but assisted by nations such as Britain and Australia. On 14 August 1945, US General Douglas MacArthur assumed the role of military governor of Japan. MacArthur's main aims as governor were to destroy Japan's military capability and establish a Western-style democracy.

The aftermath of war

Under the terms of surrender, Japan had to accept a constitution which forbade the possession of any significant armed forces. All that was left of the Japanese army, navy and airforce was destroyed. The Allied forces established courts to carry out swift justice against those who did not accept the new order, as well as to control any lawlessness in the aftermath of war. Some Japanese were tried as war criminals.

◀ **Imposing law and order**
A British-run court in occupied Japan. Courts were established to ensure swift punishment for anyone challenging the Allied forces.

▼ **Feeding the people of Tokyo**
A workman handing out flour rations in Tokyo, February 1946. The USA implemented a massive programme of food aid to deal with the high levels of poverty in Japan after the war.

Winning the peace

The Allied nations were keen to get Japan back on its feet quickly. They wanted to ensure that the Japanese did not resent the occupying forces, and wanted to encourage them to realise how generous the new system could be.

Although he was a military leader in charge of an occupying force, General MacArthur established laws to give men and women equal legal rights, as well as the right to vote. The occupying forces also shared out farming land among poor families. Despite the humiliation of defeat, the Japanese rapidly took up the challenge of rebuilding their country.

Keeping the emperor

Some Allied leaders thought that Emperor Hirohito should be imprisoned or executed for inspiring the Japanese war effort. Instead, the emperor was allowed to remain Japan's official head of state, but without any real power. By not humiliating Hirohito, and using him in the new system of government, the Allies ensured that the Japanese would not turn against them.

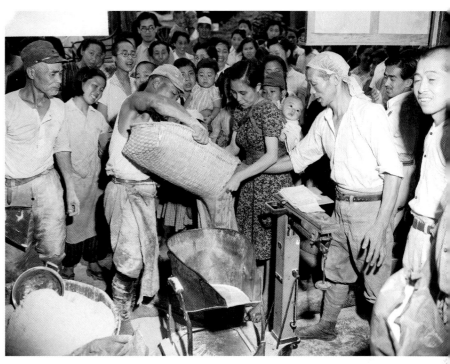

◀ **Submarine graveyard**
Dismantled Japanese submarines lie in a naval base in Kuro, Japan. A condition of surrender was that Japan would destroy all its military equipment.

▶ **The emperor meets the people**
Emperor Hirohito visits Kanagawa-Ken, Japan, February 1946. After the war, Hirohito wore civilian clothes and met ordinary Japanese people for the first time.

THE SURVIVORS

▶ Burns victim
A survivor from Nagasaki reveals the growths, called keloids, across his back. The keloids have grown over the scars caused by burns from the nuclear blast.

▼ Shocked survivors
This photograph of a woman and child was taken almost a month after the bomb was dropped. The haunted expressions on their faces demonstrate the massive shock felt by survivors.

Many who survived the initial blasts in Hiroshima and Nagasaki found their troubles were only just beginning. The full effects of the atom bombs did not become clear until the survivors started to fall ill with radiation sickness, about ten days later. They suffered vomiting and diarrhoea, their hair fell out and they lost their resistance to disease. By the end of August 1945, thousands who survived the blasts had died.

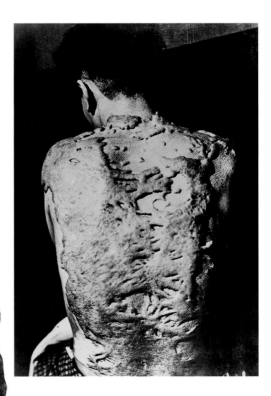

In areas around Hiroshima and Nagasaki many pregnant women lost their babies, or gave birth to children with abnormalities.

Struggling to cope

In both cities, surviving medical staff struggled to care for the sick. This was a monumental task. Most hospitals and medical equipment were destroyed in the blasts. In Hiroshima, 65 of the city's 150 doctors were killed in the initial explosion, along with hundreds of nurses. With no special help from either the Japanese or the American governments, the cities of Hiroshima and Nagasaki had to care for their survivors as best they could. Many people died who might have been saved by swift medical attention.

The hibakusha

The survivors became known in Japan as the hibakusha. As they grew stronger they formed self-help groups, and campaigned for help with their health problems. Their burns often required years of treatment and, as a result of their exposure to radiation, many developed cancers, in particular leukaemia. Some children who were born years later showed signs of radiation-related illnesses or deformities.

Finally, in 1957, the Japanese government gave the hibakusha free medical care. In 1968, the government began to grant the survivors special payments to compensate for their suffering. Many people, however, received nothing at all. (The USA did not give any money directly to the hibakusha.)

▲ Back to school
Teachers and children in a bombed-out classroom in Hiroshima, July 1946. Despite the massive devastation, within a year many schools in Hiroshima had been re-established.

▲ Rebuilding Hiroshima
(Top) This photograph of Hiroshima was taken in 1947. Although the city now looked more like a frontier town than the industrial centre it had been before the attack, within two years its inhabitants had managed to rebuild 65 per cent of the city's buildings.

HIROSHIMA TODAY

When the first journalists arrived in Hiroshima in September 1945, they described it as dead and silent. Because of the contamination, scientists feared that nothing would grow in the area for decades. However, within a few months, plants had sprung to life, and the people of Hiroshima set about the reconstruction of their city.

Across Japan, people threw themselves into work, building up the country's industrial strength. By the mid-1950s, ten years after the end of the war, Japan was at the forefront of modern manufacturing industry. By the end of the 20th century it was one of the world's leading economies.

Remembering the bomb

Hiroshima today seems like an ordinary city, with a population of over a million going about their business. Yet many survivors believe it is important for people to learn about the bomb – why it was dropped, as well as its effects. To help this, kataribe (storytellers) visit schools to teach children the events of 6 August 1945.

▲ A decade later
A shopping arcade in Hiroshima, 1954. Nearly ten years after the bomb, Hiroshima was still not back to normal. However, this vast shopping arcade under a metal roof is an example of the engineering skills which helped the Japanese economy to grow after the war.

► The Hiroshima Holocaust Study Centre
The Centre runs educational seminars about the Holocaust – the attempt by the Nazis to destroy the Jews in Europe. Like the Jews, the people of Hiroshima live with the memory of thousands in their community being killed.

Preserving buildings

Unlike many other cities that have been shattered by war, Hiroshima has preserved several of its ruined buildings. This is not because the buildings were ancient or beautiful, but so that they can stand as a memorial and a reminder of how they came to be destroyed. In 1955, the Peace Museum and Peace Park opened in Hiroshima to commemorate the bombing. Each year on 6 August, Hiroshima Day, ceremonies are held to remember the victims, the survivors and the horror of the atom bomb.

▲ **Hiroshima, 2001**
The domed concrete trade centre (on the left) is in Hiroshima's Peace Park. It was one of the few buildings in the city left standing after the bomb blast.

◄ **Peace Park**
The Hiroshima Peace Park is a place of pilgrimage and contemplation for survivors and visitors.

WAS IT THE RIGHT DECISION?

▲ **The effects of the bomb**
A survivor of the blast in Hiroshima shows the deformities on her hands in 1965, twenty years after the bomb. At the time the bomb was used, there was a lot of uncertainty about its long-term effects.

▼ **US soldiers in Vietnam, 1967**
The atom bomb was not used in the Vietnam War (1965-73), despite the length of the conflict. Some people argue that the horrific effects of the atom bombs in Japan has prevented their use in subsequent wars.

Even as the decision was being made to use the atom bombs, some high-ranking military leaders felt it was the wrong course of action. General Dwight Eisenhower, Supreme Commander of the Allied Forces in Europe, was one of them. Eisenhower's view was that, by August 1945, Japan was ready to surrender, that an Allied invasion would not be necessary, and that the USA should not have used such a horrifying weapon.

Ending the war?

It is undeniable that dropping the atom bombs did bring the Second World War and all its bloody battles to a sudden end. Some wartime Japanese politicians have said that, without the attacks on Hiroshima and Nagasaki, the peacemakers of Japan would never have persuaded the strong military leaders to stop the war.

Others argue that, if the USA had made it clear that Emperor Hirohito could stay on the throne, Japan would have surrendered and the bombs would not have been necessary. Some people feel that the USA did not think hard enough about the suffering the bombs would bring.

Scientists and the bomb

Even before the bombs were dropped, some Manhattan Project scientists expressed their concerns about the USA using a weapon of such destructive power. Many scientists have since formed groups, such as the Pugwash Conference (named after its first meeting place, in Pugwash, Canada), against the spread of nuclear weapons. Albert Einstein is said to have commented that, had he known that his theories would lead to the atom bomb, he would have become a locksmith instead.

▲ **Anti-nuclear protest, Chile, 1995**
These Chileans are protesting against French nuclear tests on the Pacific island of Mururoa. Since the war, many protest groups have campaigned against the continuing development of nuclear weapons.

▼ **Arlington National Cemetery, USA**
This military cemetery, near Washington, DC, is a reminder of the casualties of war. One of the reasons the USA used the atom bomb in 1945 was to prevent further casualties in the war against Japan.

WORLD PEACE POSTPONED

As the Second World War finally ended, people around the world had cause for both hope and fear. On the one hand, 1945 saw the birth of the United Nations, an international organisation that aimed to promote cooperation between nations and prevent another global war – and the horrors seen, for example, in the Holocaust and at Hiroshima.

On the other hand, distrust between the USA and the USSR continued to grow. Both countries competed for world resources and spent ever more money developing their armies and nuclear weapons. Because they did not fight each other directly, this was called the Cold War.

▲ **Anti-nuclear protest, Germany, 1959**
The German preacher, Martin Niemöller (centre right), and others protest against nuclear testing. Both the German and Japanese governments supported the anti-nuclear movement.

▼ **Nuclear missiles, Moscow, 1966**
The Soviet military parade their weapons in front of a crowd. As the Cold War progressed, both the USA and the USSR hoped that displays of power such as this would prevent the other side from using its nuclear weapons.

FALLOUT SHELTER

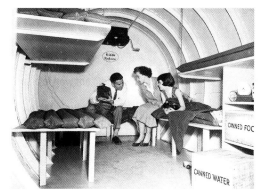

◄ **Nuclear shelter and warning sign**
A family sit in a nuclear bomb shelter in New York, USA, in 1955. (Far left) Signs directed people to the nearest public shelters. Throughout the Cold War, many Americans feared a nuclear attack from the USSR could happen at any time.

The hydrogen bomb

By the early 1950s, both sides in the Cold War had taken nuclear technology one stage further by developing the hydrogen bomb. Unlike the atom bomb, which works on the principle of nuclear fission (see pages 6 and 46), the hydrogen bomb relies on fusing the nuclei of atoms together. This process, known as nuclear fusion, created bombs many times more powerful than those used in 1945. Yet as the USA's and the USSR's weapons became ever more deadly, so each side became increasingly afraid of the other.

Anti-nuclear protests

By the 1970s, the USA and the USSR had enough nuclear weapons to destroy the world several times over. Each side hoped that, by demonstrating how powerful they were, the other would not dare to make the first move. All around the world, people set up disarmament movements, which called on governments to destroy their nuclear weapons, and protested against nuclear testing. The disarmament movement received strong support from both Germany and Japan, two nations that had learned the painful costs of total warfare.

▼ **Japanese anti-nuclear protest, 1957**
Protestors outside the British Embassy in Tokyo speak out against Britain's first-ever hydrogen bomb tests on the Christmas Islands in the Pacific.

...AND TOMORROW?

▶ **Nuclear arms treaty**
US president Ronald Reagan and Soviet leader Mikhail Gorbachev sign the Intermediate-Range Nuclear Forces Treaty, 1988. By signing the treaty, both countries agreed to destroy all their medium-range nuclear missiles.

In the late 1980s, the USA and the USSR agreed to start dismantling many of their nuclear weapons. Then, in 1991, the USSR collapsed and the Cold War finally came to an end. Many people who grew up under the shadow of the nuclear bomb in the 1950s and 1960s heaved a sigh of relief that the world would not be destroyed by an accidental tit-for-tat conflict between the world's superpowers.

Dangerous new world

However, once a new technology has been developed, it is impossible to "un-learn" it. At first, only a few countries possessed nuclear weapons – the USA, the USSR, Britain, France and China. But, by the start of the 21st century, they had spread to other countries, including India, Pakistan and Israel. The more countries there are possessing nuclear bombs, the greater the risk of at least one of them being used. In addition, many people fear that nuclear weapons could fall into the hands of terrorist groups. The terrorist attacks on the USA in September 2001 showed the destruction such groups can cause.

Hiroshima's legacy

Today, many organisations – in particular the United Nations – devote immense effort to creating dialogue between nations to prevent the use of nuclear weapons. However, perhaps the greatest deterrent to their use is the legacy of Hiroshima and Nagasaki. In all the conflicts since 1945, no one has resorted to nuclear bombs. The fate of those two cities showed the world the horror of nuclear warfare, and why it should never be experienced again.

▼ ▶ War and peace in Space
(Below) In a spirit of co-operation, US
and Russian astronauts work together on
board the Kennedy-Mir Space Station.
(Right) Protestors object to the USA's plans
to use space technology to develop its
"Star Wars" nuclear defence programme.

▲ ▶ Nuclear threat in India and Pakistan
(Above) The blast site after a nuclear test by India in
Rajasthan, western India, 1998. It looks strikingly similar
to the site of the first atom bomb test (see page 16).
(Right) A demonstrator in New Delhi, India, days after the
test. India and Pakistan both tested nuclear weapons
during their conflict over the ownership of Kashmir.

KEY DATES

1939
2 August Einstein warns President Roosevelt about the power of nuclear energy.
3 September Start of the Second World War.

1940
22 September Japan invades Indochina.
27 September Japan allies itself with Germany and Italy.

1941
21 February Japan warns Britain not to reinforce troops in Asia.
6 December President Roosevelt establishes Manhattan Project.
7 December Japanese attack Pearl Harbor. USA enters the war.
10 December Japanese advance on Malaya and Philippines.
25 December Japanese conquer Hong Kong.

1942
15 February Japanese conquer Singapore.
5 April Japanese bomb Ceylon (Sri Lanka).
18 April Americans bomb Tokyo.
2 May Japanese conquer Burma.
7 June Battle of Midway. USA inflicts heavy losses on Japan.
8 June Japanese bomb Sydney, Australia.
December British and American counter-offensive fully underway.
2 December Enrico Fermi produces the first sustained nuclear fission reaction.

1943
Island-to-island fighting. Heavy losses on both sides.
24 January President Roosevelt demands Japan's "unconditional surrender".

15 March Los Alamos site established in the New Mexico desert.

1944
15 June US bombers start a heavy bombardment of Japanese cities.
26 August Scientists warn about the need for international controls on the atom bomb.

1945
12 February Allied leaders meet at Yalta and agree a strategy for the defeat of Japan.
10 March Tokyo devastated by firebombing.
18 March All Japanese schools closed. All Japanese people over six years of age ordered to participate in the war effort.
12 April President Roosevelt dies in office. He is succeeded by his vice-president, Harry S. Truman.
8 May VE Day (Victory in Europe Day).
21 June US win 83-day-long battle for Okinawa; 12,000 American and 100,000 Japanese dead.
16 July USA carries out the first atom bomb test at Alamogordo (the "Trinity test").
26 July Allied leaders meeting in Potsdam demand Japanese unconditional surrender, with the threat of "prompt and utter destruction".
6 August Atom bomb dropped on Hiroshima.
9 August Atom bomb dropped on Nagasaki.
15 August Japan surrenders. VJ Day (Victory in Japan Day).
29 October Stalin orders a crash programme to develop atom bombs for the USSR.

GLOSSARY

Allies
The collective name given to the countries that fought against Nazi Germany and its allies, primarily Britain, France and the USA.

Atom
The smallest piece of an element, made up of electrons, protons and neutrons in different proportions. The forces required to hold these particles together are very powerful indeed.

Atom Bomb (A-bomb)
A new kind of bomb, developed during the Second World War. Whereas conventional bombs detonate by means of explosives, atom bombs use the power within atoms.

Axis Powers
The collective name given to the coalition fighting on the side of Nazi Germany, primarily Germany, Italy and Japan.

Chain Reaction
When fission causes the release of neutrons in an atom that in turn cause further fission. This chain reaction is the basis of both nuclear power and atom bombs.

Cold War
The period from the 1950s to the late 1980s when the USA and the USSR confronted each other across the globe, racing to control the most powerful weapons technology. During this period, people lived in fear of a sudden, even a mistaken, nuclear attack which could have engulfed the world.

Fission
The process by which the first atom bombs were made. In fission, atoms are split and so release the energy that binds them together.

Fusion
Later nuclear bombs used fusion, the same kind of nuclear activity that gives the Sun its energy. In fusion, atoms are brought together in different combinations, and in the process release energy.

Hydrogen Bomb (H-bomb)
A later type of nuclear bomb that used fusion rather than fission to generate explosive energy.

Nuclear Deterrent
The threat of a nuclear counter-attack which discourages acts of aggression by other countries for fear of unleashing irresistible destruction on themselves.

Nucleus (plural "nuclei")
The central core of an atom, consisting of various numbers of protons and neutrons, bound together by a very strong force.

USSR
Union of Soviet Socialist Republics. Also known as the "Soviet Union", and popularly as "Russia". The USSR competed with the USA for about fifty years after the end of the Second World War, during the Cold War, until it collapsed in the 1990s.

WHO'S WHO

Albert Einstein (1879-1955) A German physicist who won the Nobel Prize in 1921 (but not for his most famous work, the theory of relativity). Einstein transformed scientific thinking about how atoms and particles work and changed the way we think about Space. Being a Jew, he was denounced by the Nazis when they came to power in 1933 and he moved to the USA. In 1939, he heard about the work being done in Germany on splitting the atom and wrote to President Roosevelt urging him to start work on developing an atom bomb. From his prompting, the Manhattan Project was born.

Enrico Fermi (1901-54) An Italian physicist who won the Nobel Prize in 1938 for his work on radioactivity. He escaped Fascist Italy just before the war and emigrated to the USA where he continued his research on uranium, one of the most radioactive elements. On 2 December 1942, he succeeded in creating a sustained nuclear chain reaction through fusion, which paved the way for a workable atom bomb.

Emperor Hirohito (1901-89) Hirohito became emperor in 1926 at a time when it was still Japanese tradition to revere the emperor as a god. After Japan's surrender in 1945, though Hirohito remained on the throne, his godlike status was formally renounced and he became a constitutional monarch, not interfering in the political life of the country. Hirohito himself always claimed that even before the war he did not control his country's policies, but many people dispute this.

Douglas MacArthur (1880-1964) A veteran of the First World War, MacArthur became commanding general of US forces in the Far East in 1941, and from Australia helped to organise the counter-offensive against the Japanese. After the atom bombs were dropped, MacArthur formally accepted the Japanese surrender. President Truman appointed him head of the Allied occupation of Japan, where he took control of postwar Japan's reconstruction along the lines of a modern democratic state.

Robert Oppenheimer (1904-67) An American physicist responsible for directing the Manhattan Project. He and his team developed the atom bomb far more quickly than might have been achieved in peacetime. After the war, he warned against the development of the hydrogen bomb and was stripped for a time of his special security status.

Franklin D.Roosevelt (1882-1945) President of the USA for a record four terms. An attack of polio in 1921 left him in a wheelchair. He first became president in 1932, during the Great Depression, and instituted a radical programme of poverty relief and national reconstruction called the New Deal. When the Second World War started in 1939, he backed Britain but kept the USA out of the war until Japan attacked Pearl Harbor in 1941. Roosevelt authorised the development of the atom bomb but died in office in April 1945, just a few months before the first bomb was used.

Joseph Stalin (1879-1953) Originally called Djugashvili, he changed his name to Stalin ("man of steel") and in 1924 became leader of the Soviet Union. Stalin's attempts to modernise the Russian economy caused millions to die of famine; millions more were executed when they failed to meet unrealistic targets. Stalin made a pact with Hitler which was broken when Hitler invaded the USSR, and Stalin was forced to side with the Allies. Tens of millions of Soviet soldiers and civilians died in the Second World War, but by the end of the conflict the USSR was a world superpower alongside the USA. As the war ended, the two superpowers raced each other to achieve maximum influence over different parts of the world. The US decision to drop the atom bombs and take control of defeated Japan was a major blow to Stalin's ambitions in Asia.

Harry S. Truman (1884-1972) Truman had served only 82 days as Roosevelt's vice-president when Roosevelt died and Truman became president of the USA. Within months he was faced with the decision about whether or not to drop the atom bombs on Japan. Immediately after the war, Truman showed himself to be a liberal and a conciliator, trying to ensure rapid reconstruction of the defeated Axis countries and their redevelopment as Western democracies, to counterbalance the growing influence of the USSR.

THE SCIENCE

Nuclear power

Atoms are made up of many different "sub-atomic" particles. The largest of them, and the ones best understood at the time the atom bomb was developed, are neutrons, electrons and protons. The protons and neutrons lie in the core (the "nucleus") of the atom while the electrons circle around it. Since all protons are positively charged, in theory they should repel each other – as do the similar poles of a magnet. Scientists realised that there must be a very strong force holding the protons together. They called it "strong nuclear force". It is this force that keeps most elements stable and stops them from falling apart.

Radioactivity

Some elements, or some versions ("isotopes") of elements, are unstable. This means that they are constantly leaking energy. Such elements are said to be "radioactive" and they give off nuclear radiation.

Chain reaction

Just before the Second World War, scientists discovered that one isotope of uranium, uranium 235, could be split fairly easily by firing a stream of neutrons into its nucleus. When the nucleus splits, it breaks into two and a few neutrons escape. Some of these sometimes collide with more uranium 235 atoms and split those, thereby creating a chain reaction. Each time this splitting happens, it releases more of the strong nuclear force. This splitting of atoms is called "fission" and was the technology behind the first atom bombs. (When this fission is controlled or slowed down it can be used for nuclear power. When used in nuclear bombs it is allowed to multiply in an uncontrolled way.)

In July 1941, British scientists calculated that a nuclear weapon could be made using just 10 kilograms of uranium 235. This isotope is so unstable that sufficient neutrons break away naturally to start a chain reaction of their own accord. The amount of uranium (or other element) required to cause a chain reaction is called the "critical mass". The chain reaction results in a huge build-up of energy.

How the bombs worked

The "Little Boy" bomb dropped on Hiroshima used uranium 235. Conventional explosives were used to fire one piece of uranium 235 into another. This gave rise to a huge and rapid chain reaction until the energy produced exploded as a bomb.

The "Fat Man" bomb dropped on Nagasaki used plutonium 239, an isotope of another radioactive element discovered in 1941. Because plutonium is so radioactive, too many neutrons would have leaked from it before the chain reaction could create the maximum blast, so this bomb needed a different design.

In the Fat Man bomb, explosives were packed round a hollow piece of plutonium in a shell of uranium. When the explosives were detonated, they exploded inward into the radioactive material. This exerted vast force on it and crushed it into a very dense mass, sufficient to start a chain reaction.

The effects of an atom bomb

The first effect of a nuclear bomb is the blast itself. This varies according to the size of the bomb (usually measured in the equivalent of thousands of tons of conventional explosives) and also the height at which it is detonated.

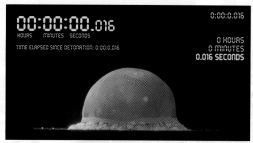

The explosion creates a huge shock wave which crushes objects in its path, and extremely powerful and destructive winds. The higher in the sky a bomb is exploded, the greater its shock wave. The nearer the ground it is detonated, the larger the crater it creates. The debris dug out of the ground by the explosion is blasted high in the air and eventually falls back to earth as radioactive "fallout".

The second effect of a nuclear bomb is the intense heat released by the explosion, called "thermal radiation". People 10 km away from Hiroshima and Nagasaki were severely burned. These burns can give rise to such physical shock that many die as a result. People also die of asphyxiation as the air is sucked up into the vacuum created by the nuclear blast.

These effects are basically similar to a conventional bomb magnified many thousands of times. In addition, there are the effects of the nuclear radiation emitted by the blast. It is not altogether clear exactly what damage was done by this first dose of radiation to the survivors of Hiroshima and Nagasaki, but most experts believe that even small doses of radiation can have harmful effects for many years to come.

Radioactive fallout

The heat of the nuclear blast is so great that it burns up the available oxygen and creates a vacuum. This sucks into itself all the debris flying around, which is then thrown up into the air. There it is spread out by a process of convection, so creating the characteristic "mushroom cloud". All this debris, having been affected by the nuclear blast, is dangerously radioactive. As the radioactive dust falls back down to the ground, it causes its own damage.

The top of the mushroom cloud can extend for a considerable distance, and air currents can carry the dust still farther. Wherever it eventually falls, it contaminates the ground itself, the water, the livestock and the people on whom it lands.

As with the effects of direct nuclear radiation, while we do not know for sure the full extent of the damage caused by radioactive fallout, we do know that it is damaging to both health and natural processes, and can give rise to a wide range of mutations and birth defects.

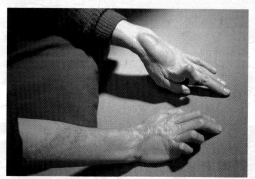

Several areas in the world where nuclear weapons were tested have remained contaminated and dangerous to life for many decades afterwards. For the same reason, disposing of the waste produced by nuclear power stations presents the world with a real problem: any leakage from the waste could potentially create extensive and long-lasting damage.

INDEX

Acknowledgments

Design
M&M Design Partnership

Photo research
Diana Morris

Photographs
AKG Images: front cover main image, 2-3, 7t, 13r,14-15,14cr,15br,17c, 18tr, 24-25, 25b, 26b, 28b, 29t, 30b, 31t, 40t, 45tl, 45bl, 46br.
F. Arias/Sipa/Rex Features: 39t.
Nigel Barklie/Rex Features: 43tr.
Bettmann/Corbis: front cover br, 1, 11cr, 16br, 20t, 22t, 33c, 33b, 34bl, 35t, 35b, 36t, 38t, 38b, 41tc, 45c, 47cr.
Horace Bristol/Corbis: 21t.
Jewgeni Chaldej/AKG Images: 19b.
Corbis: 4bl, 6tr, 10-11, 11b, 13bl, 16tl, 16bl, 22-23, 29c, 29b, 34cr, 47tl.
Robert Essel NYC/Corbis: 37t.
Holocaust Education Center, Hiroshima: 37b.
Hulton/Corbis: back cover, 27b, 46-47.
Hulton Archive: 10b.
Wally McNamee/Corbis: 42t.
William Manning/Corbis: 39b.
NASA: 4-5.
Peter Newark's Pictures: 6bl, 8cl, 8br, 9t, 13tl, 20b, 30t, 45br.
The New York Times/Peter Newark's Pictures: 24br.
Popperfoto: 12b, 25tr, 26c, 27b, 28t, 31b, 32b, 33t, 40b, 41b, 43tl, 46cr.
Reuters/Popperfoto: 15cl, 19tl, 43bl, 43br.
David Samuel Robbins/Corbis: 37b.
Sipa/Rex Features: 5tr.
UNSCOM/Sygma/Corbis: 5br.
US Air Force/Courtesy Smithsonian/Reuters/Popperfoto: 23c.
Melvin Weiss/AKG Images: 18b.

Every attempt has been made to clear copyright. Should there be any inadvertent omission, please apply to the publisher for rectification.